Whispers of the Soul

Whispers of the Soul

A Collection of poetry and works by

REETU GUPTA

When you are silent,

your soul whispers words of love to you.

Do not wait. Surrender to this love, for there comes a time when nothing is more meaningful than surrendering to Love.

© 2025 Reetu Gupta

All rights reserved. No part of this book may be reproduced or used in any manner without the prior written permission of the copyright owner, except for the use of brief quotations in a book review.

To request permissions, contact the author.

Printed in the United States of America.
First edition February 2025.

Cover and layout design by G Sharp Design, LLC.
www.gsharpmajor.com

ISBN 979-8-9912674-1-0 (paperback)
ISBN 979-8-9912674-2-7 (ebook)

To the ones who are in search of Love,
this book is dedicated to you.

Because the love you are searching
for is within you.

You are that Love.

Dear Lovely Reader,

You are the love that you seek. You are the light.
This book is not meant to be read from cover to cover.
Rather, it is meant to speak to you in whatever way
you so choose.

Maybe you read it backward, maybe you pick a topic of
Love and start there, or maybe you close your eyes and ask
the universe, "What is my message today?"

Open to a random page and feel the magic.

As you read through these works, my wish is that you
realize and understand the only love you need is within
you. It is YOU.

May you become the love that you are looking for, and
may this love find you in all things.

Reetu

TABLE OF CONTENTS

1	Love & Faith	1
2	Love & Joy	25
3	Love & Mysticism	49
4	Love & Passion	85
5	Love & Purpose	113
6	Love & Gratitude	139
7	Love & Courage	149
8	Love & Alchemy	157
9	Love & Poetry	173
	References	197

1

Love
& Faith

MY PRAYER ANSWERED

"I asked for Strength,

God gave me difficulties to face.

I asked for Wisdom,

God gave me problems to solve.

I asked for Courage,

God gave me danger to overcome.

I asked for Love,

God gave me troubled people to help.

I asked for Favors,

God gave me opportunities.

I received nothing I wanted;

I received everything I needed.

My PRAYER has been answered."

Author unknown

LOVE & FAITH

As you start your day today, I would like you to carry three simple things with you:

Faith, Love, and Courage.

Have faith in yourself and in your abilities.

Have faith in a guiding force that you are exactly where you are meant to be.

Have a deep love for yourself and all your unique qualities. There is no one like you.

Have a love for those around you and an understanding that everyone has their own path.

Have the courage to believe you are exactly where you need to be.

When I speak of faith, it does not always mean faith in God. Faith means having faith in a force stronger than you, having faith that you are guided, having faith in yourself, and having faith in your abilities.

You are worthy of love.

Tell yourself,

I love you,

I am worthy of love,

I love you,

I deserve to love and be loved.

When you have love for yourself, it attracts the
same pure love into your life.

Having love for yourself means you are honest with yourself; thus you are also honest with others.

Having love for yourself means you are loyal to yourself; thus you are also loyal to others.

Having love for yourself means you respect and hold yourself to a high standard; thus you also treat others with this same love and respect.

When you have love for yourself, it automatically becomes the love you seek in others you attract this pure love, and you allow this pure love into your heart and your life.

Become the love you seek. Begin by simply telling yourself, I am worthy of love. I already love you.

Faith makes it possible.

Surrender makes it graceful.

Love makes it beautiful.

Fear says, run. Run to a place where growth is not required of you. A place where we are safe. Hide.

Heart says, love. Love more. Love once again. You are courageous and stronger than you know. Allow continual transformation.

In Search of Love...

We are all in search of love in some way—love in a partner or the partner itself, love from a family member, or the love of what you do in life that brings out your spark. To find this love, you must become this love. To become this love, love without fear, hesitation, or expectation. Love fully. And express the truth that's in your heart. When you do this, you will feel that spark. Do this, and you will not only radiate a loving energy but you will attract it also!

Love Without Hesitation

To say, "I love you if," or, "I will love you when," we place a condition on our love and this removes the love itself, as the interaction has now become a transaction. We are left with an emotion that is insecurely based upon conditions.

When we can love without hesitation and expectation, when we love without fear nor condition, it is then we truly love for the sake of loving.

As love radiates from you, the same energy is attracted your way.

Your soul is lit up and your heart smiles from within!

To love without regret,

to love without what-ifs,

to love without hesitation,

expectation,

or condition,

is to love purely, authentically, and sincerely.

This love has endured inside you

with neither beginning nor end.

Give all to love, because love cannot fail.

In love and with love, love will endure,

Because,

to Love

is

to Live

Ego speaks,

love listens.

Ego takes,

love gives.

Ego says *you must fit into my schedule.*
Love says *my love for you is timeless.*

Ego says *I need.*
Love says *what do you need?*

Ego is selfish, working only within the 'I.'
Love is caring and thoughtful.

Ego will lie, cheat, and steal to get through life.
Love is truthful, honest, and filled with integrity.

Ego is insecure, weak, and lacks compassion.
Love is strength, faith, and devotion.

You can choose to lose love, because of ego.
Or lose your ego, for the sake of love.

Every breath you take is an opportunity to inhale love,

And exhale Love.

Love as much as you Breathe.

Surround yourself with people who

lift you

support you

love you, and

encourage you.

Because when the company you keep helps you in this way, it will

elevate you to new heights.

Choose to surround yourself with the people who

support you on your journey.

Who will stand with you through the storm and break into applause as you run through the finish line and come out the other side triumphantly so.

These are the chosen ones who will be the guiding light on your path to achieving your true destiny.

Be with the dreamers, the believers, and the lovers, because they will stand with you and be the force you need to make your dreams come true.

Love is as simple as your heartbeat and as beautiful as a fragrant breeze.

Love is always within you, embrace it.

There is only one truth that will always prevail in life, without failure, without exception:

love.

Love endures and will always prevail.

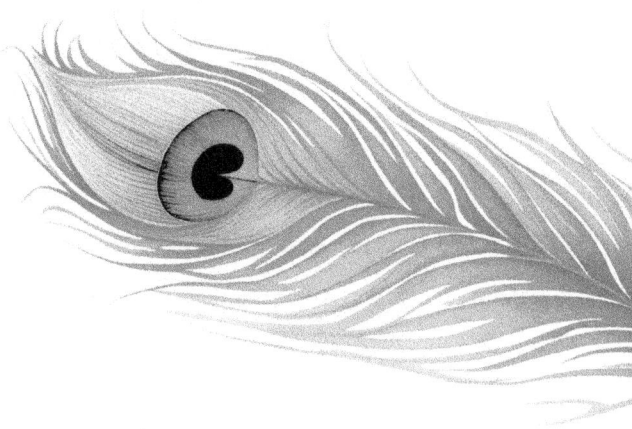

It is love that is all you truly seek.

Everything you experience is love seeking you.

When you live life authentically,

unapologetically,

enthusiastically,

as You,

There is no competition.

Because there is no one like you.

You are rare.

When you live life as your most authentic self,

When you choose to live life as the best version of yourself,

You will feel a deep sense of freedom,

An exhilarating sense of joy.

Embrace the rarity that is You.

The greatest gift

to those we love

is to listen with compassion.

Compassionate listening is not just hearing the words but the ability to make the person feel your presence. When you practice this, you are giving pure love and in turn will receive the same.

As Buddhism suggests, the past is complete, and the future is not yet here. The only moment that matters is this moment right now. And this moment is overflowing with love, possibility, magic, and dreams. Embrace this moment with all you have.

I long to speak the love that's in my heart and have it cherished as so.

Love should not be left unspoken. It is meant to be set free.

True love cherishes the love given and holds it close to its heart.

True love knows that love is rare and protects it at all costs.

True love cares deeply, genuinely, and unconditionally.

True love is honest and devoted, choosing truth, respect, and loyalty.

Anything less than this is not truth in love, it is love without truth.

True love endures as it carries every virtue with it along the way.

The surest sign of
strength is how gently,
honestly, and purely
you love.

We need not look for love; we simply must become love. And then, magically and unexpectedly, it finds you along the way.

Love cannot exist where the ego lives.

Love will not survive where there is selfish desire.

Where there is joy, happiness, gratitude, truth, kindness, laughter, inspiration, and passion—therein lies love.

When you become joyful, full of gratitude and kindness,

when you can smile at the small things,

and laugh at everything,

you emit love.

Love will then seek you.

A heart that is pure has many virtues.

Loyalty is a rare, beautiful trait of pure love.

Pure Love is a virtue of the loyal,

as loyalty is the virtue of faithfulness.

To live is to love.

To love is to be loyal.

To be loyal is to embrace true love.

The simplest of virtues are also what makes the soul the most beautiful. When you sincerely encompass loyalty and faithfulness, your soul shines with the light of pure love.

When you stand in the light of pure love, all else falls away—you become light, attract light, and become pure love.

"And now these three remain: faith, hope, and love. But the greatest of these is love."

1 Corinthians 13:13

True beauty and happiness come from being your most bona fide, spirited self.

You are the most powerful force that exists.

Embrace the fullness of You.

When our faith becomes
all love, we enter into greatness.
When we consistently come
from love, everything works
in our favor.

Be strong as thunder when it comes to your morals,

soft as the rain when you shower your love,

As tender as the music of crickets on a summer night with your kindness,

As gentle as flowers with your words,

and shine as bright as the sun in the face of your dreams

It takes courage to speak the truth that is in your heart.

Yet, your heart yearns to share this love.

Have the courage not only to love,

but to speak

and act boldly with love.

Love need not be loud.

Love in its purest form is simply loving words

from the heart.

Love takes courage and courage needs love.

"If you judge people, you have no time to love them."

Mother Theresa

We cannot see peace
where there is judgment.
We cannot see love
where there is hate.
We cannot see harmony
where there is disunity.

When we love without
judgment, this love spreads
far and wide. The more we love and
create harmony, the more others will
feel this and in turn, also spread their
love and harmony.

2

Love & Joy

"The present moment is filled
with joy and happiness,
if you are attentive,
you will see it."

Thich Nhat Hanh

If you look at the world with resentment,
all you will see is anger.

If you look at the world with sadness,
all you will experience is unhappiness.

If you look at the world with joy,
all you will see is laughter.

And when you look at the world with love,
all you will see, feel, and experience is love.

The way to bring love into your life is by only seeing love.

Life is Precious

Live with love.

Speak the love that is in your heart.

Love without condition.

Love without hesitation.

Laugh uncontrollably.

Hug warmly.

Kiss passionately.

Live with no excuses.

Love with no regret.

Live life with life.

Live life with love.

If it brings you joy,

if it makes your heart smile and laugh,

if it brings you peace,

if it makes you feel inspired,

uplifts you,

elevates you,

encourages you,

show it gratitude and keep it close.

If it brings you sadness,

if it creates questions in your heart,

if it brings feelings of negativity,

this is your soul telling you,

it is not for you.

You are meant to fly.

So set it free

and once you let go,

you will feel lighter,

and attract positivity and love.

You are meant to fly.

Surround yourself with the energy that uplifts you,

encourages you,

and inspires you to be authentically

YOU.

You are Rare.

In a world where everyone wants to be someone else,

where everyone is smiling hesitantly and posing insecurely,

choose to be sincerely and securely YOU.

The more you move towards an idea that is not yours

or chase a version of yourself that is not authentic,

the more insecurity and unhappiness you will feel.

The only thing that will ground you, and bring

you true joy,

is when embracing the genuinely raw version of YOU.

Courage helps you conquer challenges.

Love enriches your relationships.

Freedom guides you toward authenticity.

Joy illuminates the day.

And passion drives your ambitions.

When courage, love, freedom, joy, and passion unite, a future is created where each moment vibrantly affirms life.

> Be generous with your smile, even to those who do not return it.
>
> Be giving with your love, especially to those who need it most.

Do not live with regret,

know that everything happens for a reason.

Do not live with anger,

forgive without condition.

Do not live in hesitation,

take the step, make the leap, and do so with conviction.

Life becomes beautiful by change, not by chance.

Allow it and welcome change.

Do not live in the fear of 'what if,'

live in the moment of 'I will.'

Love
with your full heart.

Laugh
until your cheeks hurt.

Live
as though your heaven is on earth.

Dance
like everyone's watching.

Rise
above the suffering.

Cherish
the present moment.

Forgive, forget, and
love with no regret.

Why do we postpone feeling alive?

The only moment to be alive is right here, right now.

Do not postpone your happiness,

Choose to be joyful in the present moment.

Keep those close to you who love you for you and encourage you on your path. Do not make yourself smaller to fit into the mold created by society's perception of you. Another person's perception of you is not your reality. Embrace yourself as you are and allow yourself to live large!

Be You.

Life is much more fun this way.

Happiness is to smile at small things,

to laugh at all things,

to see the beauty in everyone,

to love with your soul,

to be filled with faith,

to be grateful,

And live a life of love.

Love is the most precious thing in the world.

It cannot be valued; it cannot be touched only felt.

It is the most precious, and yet, sometimes treated like a commodity.
Thus, the question arises: why can't we hold on to love?

Love, like a lotus, can grow through murky water and will always grow towards the light.

Love blossoms when we allow it to. Love blossoms when we become love itself.

Forgiveness is Freedom

Love and forgiveness can set us free.
Love is pure and unconditional.

Forgiveness must also be pure and unconditional.
We must not say, I love you when, or I will forgive you if.
Then we have made our love and our forgiveness
a transaction.

Love and forgiveness must be unconditional.
And when it is,
forgiveness becomes freedom.

Forgiveness is not just forgiving the other person, but it is forgiving yourself for participating.

It is gratitude, for knowing that this situation gave you a life lesson that will change and transform you.

Forgiveness is not, "I forgive you, but I will never forget." This means you have not let it go. Forgiveness is understanding that others make mistakes, showing them grace, and giving yourself the grace to let it go. Most of the time, we hold on to anger because it becomes comfortable. But once you let it go, you become free. And this space that used to be filled with anger and resentment will now be filled with joy that will attract more joy. And your heart will be set free.

You Have a Light Within You

This light wants to shine so bright.

You feel this light, you feel it when you accomplish something, big or small. Maybe you feel it when you make someone smile, maybe you feel it when you are in love, maybe you feel it when you kill it at the gym or when you get something done at work. That spark of excitement. Allow this spark to shine every day and every moment of every day.

There will be circumstances that may cause you to feel like your light is dimmed, but you have to find the strength to keep shining. Find strength in faith.

Or maybe it's the people around you who try to extinguish your light; they may try to attack your character to bring you down. No one can dim your light. If you have people around you who don't allow your light to shine, you have to rise above it and when you do, the universe brings you the people who will support and elevate you.

All you have to do is remember you are capable of achieving your dreams, and you have a light that shines so bright. Allow it. Shine so bright, and when you do, love and happiness will find you.

Fill your life with love.
Radiate this love back
to the world.

Love simply to love.

To be loved is one thing,

but to *be love*

is the source of everything.

If love was an energy, I picture it as pure laughter.

Laughter is a sign of a pure soul that is filled with joy. When you can smile and laugh, it is because your heart is filled with genuine love. Laughter is when the heart smiles and the soul dances.

When you speak pure words from the heart, a light shines from your heart into theirs and the soul glows with compassion and affection.

Love is the water of life. It nourishes our souls.

Smile because you are loved.

Smile because you are exactly where you need to be.

Smile because being unhappy is unworthy of you.

Smile. Just because.

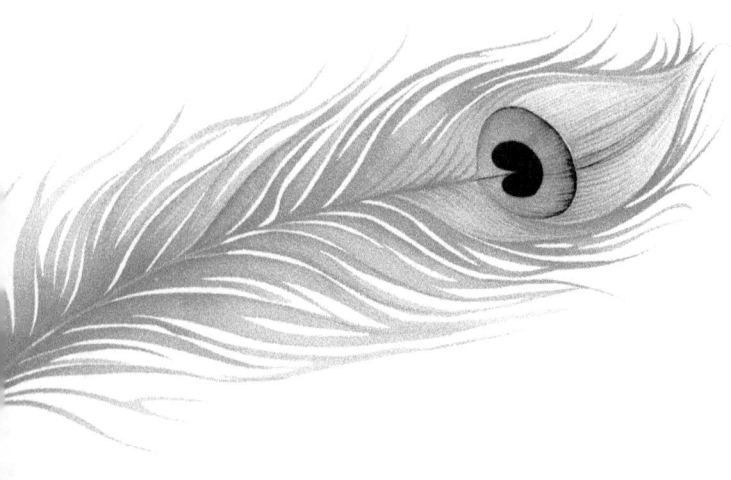

The words you tell yourself will define how your day unfolds.

Speak love into your day.

Speak life into your day.

Speak of kindness, respect, courage, and integrity, and watch your world transform.

The secret to happiness is to always continue laughing, smiling, and seeing joy in all things.

There are some souls who see joy in everything and will leave a trail of joy behind when they go.

When you can remember to laugh, play, and smile, life will be enjoyed differently. As Shakespeare said, all the world's a stage. Let's not take life so seriously and learn to laugh and smile every day. This is when joy will surround you.

To be enlightened is to be filled with light, filled with love.
Why is it that when we grow up, we forget to laugh,
to enjoy life?

It is said that enlightened souls have a childlike whimsy to them. This is because these souls have learned to see light and be light. It all starts with a smile: smile at the beginning of your day, smile through the day, and smile with gratitude at the end of the day!

When we give with our whole heart, it creates more joy and love in the world.

The Present Moment

We must not defer happiness.

We say:

I'm waiting to be happy,

I'm waiting to feel at home,

I'm waiting for the one,

I'm waiting to make the call,

I'm waiting to say I love you.

Why must we defer happiness to tomorrow? Tomorrow is that which we wait for, yet it never arrives. The only moment we truly have is the present moment.

This moment is overflowing with possibilities. This is the moment to say I love you, this is the moment to smile, this is the moment to be happy. And when you choose to be happy today, you will surely remain happy tomorrow.

3

Love & Mysticism

> "I once had a
> thousand desires,
> but in my one desire
> to know you, all else
> melted away."
>
> Rumi

I am not looking for

that first love, Love

I want that always love, Love

I want that everlasting love,

the goes-through-lifetimes kind of love.

Be weird.

Believe in magic and mystics,

and love at first sight.

Be the poet and the misfit,

And mysterious like moonlight.

They say to be subtle is to be accepted,

but subtlety is a torturous plight.

For I would rather be bold and crazy,

although to some this is fatalistic.

For me, I choose weird,

I choose free, and

I choose to be me.

She who validates herself,

empowers herself.

She who loves herself,

seeks only those who will also radiate this love.

She who empowers herself,

uplifts others.

She who uplifts herself,

seeks only those who are strong enough to accept her in all her strength.

Poetry is words written on paper
While music is poetry written on silence.
Poetry and music paint beauty into the mundane.

Music is the soundtrack to life,
Music brings life out of simplicity.
And into divinity.

Dance out loud.
Love out loud.

When the music hits my soul,
I feel free as
if I have become
the melody.

She loves from her soul

and speaks from her heart.

Fall in love with the moon,

tell secrets to the trees,

dance in the rain,

love wildly like the sun,

And play as freely as the breeze.

Live in the moment, and

love every moment you are here.

She's an old soul who loves deeply and

gives kindness generously.

She believes in magic and tells her secrets to the moon,

follows the rhythm of her heart, and the beat of her soul.

What is meant to be,

will always find its way and come to be.

Always.

What is meant for you always finds you, and

cannot pass you.

You can't fight fate.

Once you have your dream in your heart,

begin walking the path,

believe it will come true,

and the universe will step in to help you.

        I tell the moon all my secrets,

        and He tells me all about love.

I choose to live in a way where I embrace love fully,

I choose to love out loud,

I choose to live out loud,

I choose to dance out loud,

I choose to live with all the colours of love,

music, and poetry.

I simply choose to love

above all.

Be Daring.

Be Free.

Be Love.

Dream deeply, dream curiously.

Love deeply

and always

love unconditionally.

Today, may you allow your light to shine so bright.

May you listen to music and smile

and dance to the song that plays in your mind.

May you allow pure love to set your soul on fire

and set your heart free.

May you listen to your heart all day,

come what may.

May you believe in magic,

may you fall in love with love,

may you fall in love with yourself,

and may you fall in love with your life.

I am a woman, a tiger, a warrior.

I can love gently and deeply; my stripes are emblazoned with shades of fierce.

I can be woman, warrior, or tiger.
I can be all,
I can be one,
do not assume that I am none.
For I am the one who will wait in the grass for my turn
and will always
overcome.

Be fearlessly authentic.
Embrace your rarity.

Say these words out loud,

as if you are speaking to your heart,

with your hand over your heart:

> **LOVE MANTRA 1**
>
> Oh dear one, I will listen deeply to your words,
>
> I am here
>
> I trust you
>
> I protect you

Your heart whispers a truth to you... a truth you know is real... if this truth has been placed in your heart, the universe will make it happen. Your job is to have faith in yourself and take the first step.

Desire

to await what the stars shall bring.

Derived from the Latin *desiderare*, 'to long or wish for,' which itself derives from de sidere, 'from the stars.'

Desire…The wishes you have made among the moon and stars are meant to be,

meant to come

true.

Stay in faith.

> ## **LOVE MANTRA 2**
>
> I am deserving of love.
>
> The love I seek is within me.
>
> I will become the love I seek and reflect this love
> to the world.
>
> I am love.
>
> I will, first and foremost, love myself.
>
> The love I give to my own soul will radiate love to others
> and the love I seek will then embrace me.
>
> I am divine love.

You, more than anyone, are deserving of love.

Love is already written for you, already blessed, all you have to do is step forward, open your arms, and tell yourself you deserve it.

Become the love you wish for
and this love will find you
and make your wish come true.

You have the ability to write your own destiny, and the moment is right now.
This moment is overflowing with possibility,
This moment is where you hold the pen,
and you decide who you want to be.
You create your destiny.

Pure love is in the eyes, as the eyes are the window to the soul.

The eyes will always shine with the beauty of a pure soul. When you look at the one you love, your eyes will shine with true love, and their soul will stir.

When they look at you with pure love, your heart will smile and your soul will say,

that's the one.

Sometimes you can meet another person, a moment written in destiny, and in one glance, you can feel the past, present, and future.
This is the magic of love, a divine soul connection.

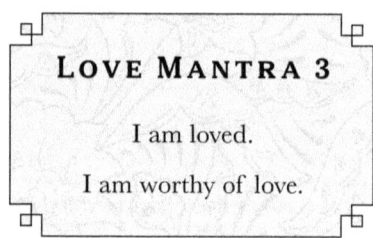

What would love do?

When you are in any situation, where you cannot seem to find a way, know that the answer is always within you. All you have to do is listen, genuinely, sincerely, and with pure intention.

Ask yourself, *What would love do?* And your heart will smile in response, and whisper the answer to you.

When you follow the path of love, love will always passionately follow you.

> ## LOVE MANTRA 4
>
> I am aware of the barriers I have built against love.
>
> I love myself; this love dissolves all barriers and allows love to flow freely.
>
> My heart is open to love, and love will renew me.

Whatever you choose to do,
do it with love and passion.

Love is my religion.
Music is my passion.
Dance is my devotion.

The power of love.

It breaks through darkness, shining like the moon and emanating with a force that the heart feels and the soul understands.

Love is the reason the moon shines.

Love is the reason the stars hang in the sky.

Love is the reason stars are wished upon and dance through the night.

Love allows us to reach for the unknown when we trust our heart.

Love removes suffering and sets us free.

Love is here only for the sake of love.

We can live without many things, but we cannot live without love.

For love is the reason for everything.

The wild woman is like a comet, fleeting, but when she appears, she bodes mischief and magic. She cannot be caught, only loved.

Love her and love her wild.

The palm tree is

born to withstand the wind.

It will bend during the wind but as soon as the storm is over, it stands right back up.

The righteous will flourish like the palm tree.

There is something magical about palm trees. As the wind dances through the palm of leaves, it seems to speak of past mysteries and stories. If you listen closely, the palm trees will reveal all their stories.

There are dreams you have when you sleep, and there are dreams that you cannot let sleep.

A dream is your heart whispering your destiny to you. These dreams are already written in the stars.

Having dreams in your heart is what keeps life passionate.

Listen to the dreams your heart speaks of, fill your heart with love, passion, and curiosity, and believe that you can achieve anything.

Two souls come together
not by chance,

but because of lifetimes of love,

because they feel the magic and

because it is written, and so it shall be.

True love is not,

I love you if, or

I love you when.

True love is,

I Love You Always.

It is love for the sake of love.

It is unconditional,
unequivocal.

It is not transactional.

It is love out loud,
spoken clearly, and
spoken from the heart.

It is love in colour.

It is love that is not in black and white
but in every colour.

Fate is believing in destiny,
the tumultuous unknown and
the passionate twin flame love
fated to meet, written in the stars.

Destiny is knowing you will meet.
Fate is waiting to meet.
Faith is surrendering to the moment.

To believe in fate

is to believe

in destiny,

in longing,

in desire and

inevitable passion for the soul.

Souls don't meet by accident.

It is the moment where destiny flirts with fate.

It was love at first laugh,

And when she laughed, he heard music
and his eyes smiled back with love.

She laughed and looked at him, seeing a Soulmate's spark
in his eyes.
He heard music in her laughter and knew this was forever.

His name is written in my personal legend, and
mine in his.

Lover and beloved.

One I seek, and one I know.

One I see, and one I call.

You will attract the same energy around you that
exists within you.

If you are full of negativity, stress, anger, and jealousy, this
is the energy that will surround you.

If you are full of love, forgiveness, joy, and kindness, you
attract purity, you attract light, you attract pure love, and
you become pure love.

Coincidence

A moment in time written just for you, where destiny shines on you and reveals its magic.

That moment where you meet another's gaze...
That elusive second where you cross paths with a certain someone...
That message of love just when you needed to hear it...
That sign that you know in your heart was meant just for you...

These instances are pre-written. It is when the divine shines only for you and says, "I'm with you," showing you a glimpse of what is meant to be. I do not believe there exists such a thing as 'just a coincidence.' Rather, it is a moment written in time just for you.

Always believe that you are exactly where you are meant to be, and be open to the divine signs from the universe. These signs are what lead your heart.

Surround yourself with women who are there to support you, not compete with you.

Surround yourself with women who will elevate you, not belittle you.

Surround yourself with women who will pray behind your back, not speak against you when your back is turned.

I believe in
mischief,
misbehaving,
and magic.

The awakened soul shines with a light that is seen and felt by others.

It illuminates the way for others, with captivating love.

Trust your intuition and believe in the magic of love…

Love is the force that ignites the spirit.
When you are silent, the whispers of your heart will arise.
Do not wait, surrender to Love.

Listen to your heart and always act with love, grace,
beauty, and kindness.

Allow your heart to speak, and allow your love to shine through your soul; this is the essence of true beauty.
A beautiful soul glows with the divine light of happiness.

The moon keeps all the secrets whispered to him by the lovers who wish upon him.
He listens silently and glows magically as if to say, "Your wishes will be granted by day."

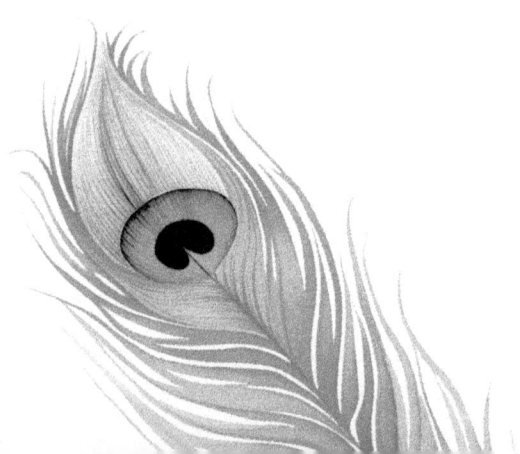

Each of us has a divine inner voice that sees with eyes that cannot see and speaks with a voice that cannot be heard. This is the voice of love, of the heart, of the soul. Follow this voice and your heart will always feel content.

It is written.

And when it is written, it is divinely planned. The universe is always with you, surrounding you with signs, showing you the way to fulfill your destiny.

Believe in love and destiny, and the universe will conspire for you.

It is written, you just have to believe. :)

4

Love & Passion

"Unless it is mad, passionate, or extraordinary love, it's a waste of your time.

There are too many mediocre things in life;

Love shouldn't be one of them."

Oscar Wilde

When love is in your heart, it needs to speak,
and once spoken, it will set you free.

Speak of the love that you carry within your soul,
without the fear of 'what if,' and
without the hesitation of 'but.' Allow your heart to
speak of love
and love will set you free.

Because the love that has been placed in your heart
has been placed there for a reason.
It has been placed there to tell you that you are
worthy of love.

Embrace love, because whatever you do with love,
whenever you speak of love and with love, this is always the
way to dreams, passion, and soul purpose.

Where does your mind go when you wander?
Where does your soul go when you daydream?
Herein lies the secret to your soul's purpose; to your destiny.

You are here
for love
because of love and
with love.
Love is your birthright.
Love is your purpose.

Love fully.
Love out loud.
Love unconditionally.

Love is accepting you for who you are.
Love is inspiring you to be more.
Love is encouraging you to be you.

No matter what they say,

love is always the way.

True love is...
The person who inspires you,
who elevates you,
who loves you unconditionally and
who loves you as YOU.

Express love openly,

love is not meant to be hidden.

It is meant to be spoken; to be felt.

Love is meant to be set free.

Become a love letter,

to yourself and others.

Speak the love that is in your heart

every single day.

If you place love as the reason for all things,

then love itself becomes the force behind everything.

Let love guide you, let love be the reason you

do everything.

This moment, the present moment, is filled with love,

happiness, and magic.

Reach it simply by being present.

Feel it simply by having a love for life itself.

Love is the reason you are here.

In every moment, be the presence of pure love.

When we love purely, deeply, and freely, anything is possible.

When you see through the eyes of love,

everything becomes love

and everything is understood through love.

There will be no room for anything that is not love.

When you love deeply

you shine brightly

and you bring the same energy right into your life.

Everything should be done with love,

the words you speak to others,

the words you tell yourself,

the path you choose to walk, and

the decisions you make.

When these are all done with the intention of love,

the universe, which was created in love, steps in to

see it through.

Will you write my name across your heart so I become your love?

I will write your name on my palm, so you become my destiny.

To fall in love, one must be free.

Is there such a thing as too much love?
The world needs more love and more kindness.

Love is what opens the heart,

love is what sparks creativity, and

love itself is passionately art

If they love you for who you are

you become the greatest version of who you can be.

We must live, speak, and do all things,

with love,

with passion,

with intention,

or not at all.

Alive

Give your time
to what makes you feel alive.

Keep those close to you
who make your heart smile
and you feel revived.

Cherish those who awaken you,
who allow your soul to dance,
and who want to see you thrive.

If it makes you feel alive
keep it, hold it, and cherish it.

Because most people are not alive,
they simply exist.
To be alive is the greatest gift of all.

If it's not worth risking anything for, it's not love.
When you know that you will risk it all for this person,
that's love.
Love is when the risks of love pale in comparison to the
thought of not having loved.

Nothing can come in the way of pure love.
Pure love is truthful, joyful, peaceful.
Pure love flows like water.

Have the courage to love.
Have the courage to pursue your dreams.
With confidence, we can find courage.
With courage, we can do anything.

Love must be spoken,

love must be shown.

Love should not remain caged in our hearts where no one hears it,

love must always be set free.

When you love deeply and purely, your soul flies to new heights.

We must love for the sake of love.

When love is real,

when it's meant to be,

when it's pure,

nothing can stop it,

because it's already written in destiny.

When your desires come into harmony with the purpose of life, this is when passion begins to spark.

Life is about happiness, love, and passion. It is about pursuing what truly makes your soul stir and your heart skip a beat.

When the spark of desire is in harmony with your soul's purpose, the flames of passion will be ignited.

There is an enchantment to the soul who loves for the sake of love. The passion for life allows the heart to ignite and the soul to glow.

Do not silence your heart. Rather, give it a pen and allow your heart to speak its secrets.
Love is meant to be expressed, and whichever words come out will become your heart's poetry.

When destiny writes something for you, it will not and cannot pass you.

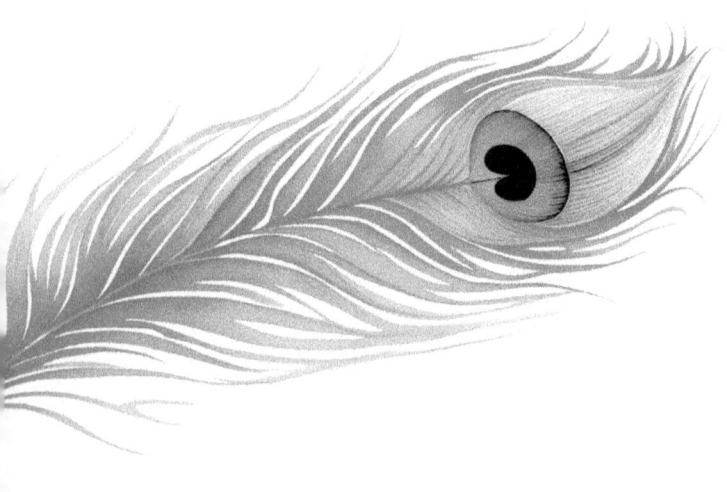

Pure love is shown by giving someone your time, your sincere presence, and your compassion.
The most precious gift you can give someone is you.

    The sun rises every day with the promise of
    shining new energy on you.

Love is an energy. It is an eternal creation, and nothing can destroy it.

The opposite of love is fear.

If we think and feel with all-encompassing love, then the opposite gets destroyed, and we are only left with love.

We need love like we need oxygen.

To love without condition,

to give without reason,

to care without expectation,

this is true love, divine love!

Love for the sake of love.

Where you are full of love, you will always be dancing to
your inner music.

When a wish is made with faith it turns into a dream…
And when you dream with passion, it can become reality.

When you have your own dreams, they will say
you are mad.
They will say, it makes no sense.
Go ahead anyway.
They will say it can't be done.
Go ahead anyway.
Do what excites your spirit.
Live mad!

In life, we are sometimes given fleeting moments of love,
but these moments give us enough love to last a lifetime.

The most important thing you can do for another is to love them just simply to love them.

Love them so they feel seen, feel heard, feel valued, and feel appreciated.

Love just to love.

Love is the essence of life.

When you can remove all the barriers you have built against love, love shines even more brightly.

We must understand that everyone, every human, has been made in the light of the universe. Thus, every person has divinity within them. But we fail to see this, and we judge others.

When we can understand that every human has a path, and has their own set of obstacles, we can see without judgment or anger; we only see with love.

When we remove all the barriers to love, we become love itself!

All we truly have is the present moment. This is the moment that matters and this moment itself is full of so much love. Embrace it.

Why are you running from your heart?
Take a moment to listen to what it has to say.
Your heart will never lead you astray.

When your passion becomes your purpose,

you shine with a light that will illuminate your path.

Follow your passion.

Follow your purpose.

Live on Purpose.

Love with Passion.

Live with Passion.

Love on Purpose.

5

Love & Purpose

> "The reward for work is not what we get,
>
> But what we become."
>
> ---
>
> Paulo Coelho

You have a purpose.

You are here for a reason.

There has been a little voice, speaking quietly to you,

guiding you in the direction of your soul's destiny.

You have a soul purpose and the universe is just waiting for you to choose to go down this path.

Your heart whispers your destiny to you, your desires.

When you listen to these words and choose to follow your heart's calling,

when you choose to follow this path with full faith,

you will see your path unfold for you as if the universe was already expecting you.

Listen to your heart,

it knows the way,

and will never lead you astray.

To be in love with yourself is the first step toward your dreams becoming reality, toward the life you desire, toward bringing the love that you crave into your life!

Love Mantra

I Can do anything I put my mind to.

I Will realize all my dreams.

I Am powerful and worthy of achieving all that I desire.

You are destined to be,
whom you choose to be.

Decide who you want to be
and allow nothing to come in the way.

Take the first step toward your dream
and the universe will guide you the rest of the way.

On the way to your dreams, you are faced with decisions that will impact your life.
It is these decisions that need to be made by you and only you, without anyone else's influence. This is the only way to achieve your dreams.

The choices you made yesterday, impact today.
And the choices you make today, impact your future.

Decide today to pursue your dreams and to make your dreams your reality.

Choose the path to your dreams.

Sometimes, we focus on impossibilities rather than transforming ourselves into becoming the possibility.

Our own thoughts create our destiny. These thoughts determine who you can be and what can be.

This moment is overflowing with what can be.
You have the ability to become exactly what you
have dreamed of.
Embrace it with all you have.

When pure love is in your heart, it guides you to do something special and meaningful in life. When you embrace this love, you embrace your soul's purpose. This purpose was whispered to your heart before you came to earth, and your heart continues to whisper it back to you.

Follow your heart.
Follow your passion.
Live with purpose.
Live your purpose.

Whatever you choose to do in life, it must be done with pure intention.

Our intention must be pure in the sense it must come from a place of positivity.

The intention should not be competition but, *I will be the best version of myself.*

The intention should be so pure that it sets your soul free.

When your intention is pure the universe steps in to help you see your dreams come true.

Reach high

for stars lie hidden in your soul.

Dream deep

for every dream precedes the goal.

Stay centered in your heart and create the life that is right for you, that speaks to you.

Trust the wisdom that is already yours, and cast aside the influences that will try to bend you uncomfortably.

You are writing your own destiny and only you know in your heart what's right for you.

What appealed to the
caterpillar will not tempt the butterfly.

Allow life's changes because
transformation is the way to make the
impossible possible and to make your
dreams your reality.

As a caterpillar, she never imagined she
could see above the trees.

As a butterfly, she can never
go back to being tied
to the ground.

Don't wait for something to happen by chance,
create the opportunity and do it by purpose.

Too often we wait, wait for the right time, wait for things to settle, wait for a moment.
Put your faith in God, in the universe, and step forward to create your destiny.
Live your life with a strong purpose and work toward
it every day.

Have a purpose.

Live with purpose.

Grab your dreams.

You can wait for your dream to come true by chance,

or make your dream come alive with purpose.

Don't trap your dreams and wait for chance.

Set your dreams free
with purpose and create your own opportunity.

Believe in your dreams
and create your destiny.

The tiger... It is my symbol, my inner narrative that whispers to me that no challenge and no upset has the ability to change who I am; my authentic self is not compromised by the dark spaces that I have to negotiate my way through. I am strength; I am virtue; I am victory.

– from *Auspicious*

Don't mistake my kindness for weakness,

My silence for subservience.

My silence is not acceptance,

My kindness is not innocence.

Kindness is compassion

Compassion is confidence

Confidence is strength

Strength is strategic.

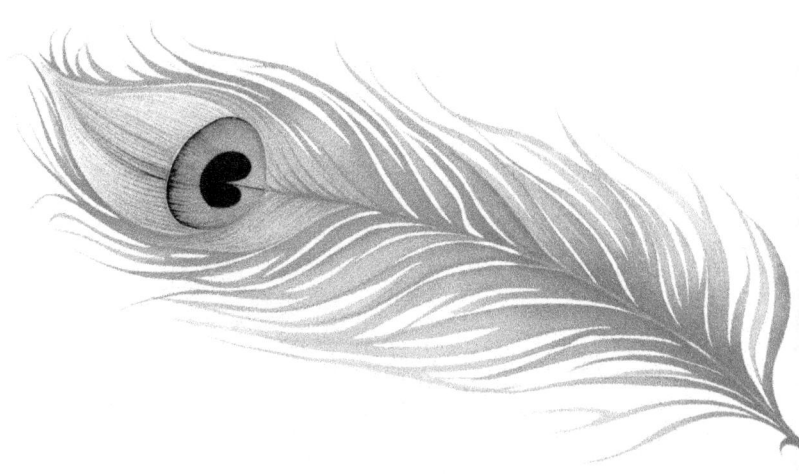

When you walk through life with a sincere purpose in your heart, those who have similar energy will find you and walk with you. I am underestimated only by those whose intentions are not pure. This energy reveals itself quickly and falls away swiftly. I have made being underestimated my superpower. When you set your intentions with kindness and the greater good, the universe will always step in and clear the path.

Every morning the sun shines with new possibilities.
Embrace what feels impossible,
Believe that You have the ability to make an impossibility, a reality.

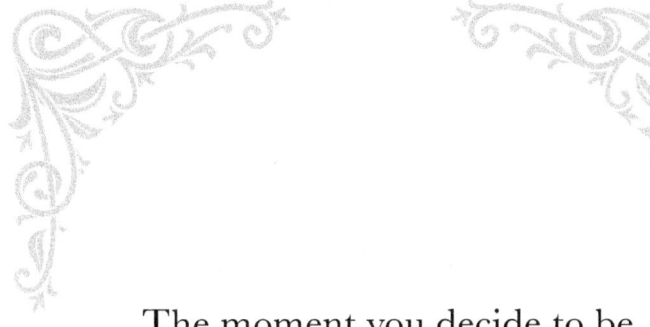

The moment you decide to be yourself, to forge your own path, is the moment you will feel happiness.

The moment you choose authenticity as opposed to duplicity you will feel the power of joy.

Duplicating the lives of others only brings sorrow and a feeling that you will never be what they are.

And this is true because you can only be you and are only destined to be you.

Everyone deserves love and respect.

When you act with integrity and truth, you create self-respect.

When you have respect for yourself, you will, in turn, treat others with respect, and they will also show you respect.

That dream you have in your heart, that secret wish, that calling, it has been given to you for a reason. It has been placed in your heart by God, by the universe. All you have to do is believe that it's possible, believe it will happen, and believe that it's already yours.

We are like the sun in this world.
We came here to bring life to everyone and be beneficial to the whole of humanity.

You search for purpose, not knowing that the purpose was given to you when you came into this world. Love. This is your only purpose.
Whether you show love with kindness,
with service, or simply with happiness
this love, this is your purpose.

The sun rises every day with the promise of shining new energy on you.

A woman does not need to fit into society's mold, nor does she need to follow a set of regulations, ultimately made by men.

A woman does not need to fit into society's mold, nor does she need to follow a set of societal norms that she never approved of to begin with.

My women, no one can tell you 'what a woman should be.'

A woman should be free to live by her own definition. That is the only acceptable end of this sentence.

Plan strategically and move silently,

love fully and share it with those who will also love you proudly.

Let your gratitude develop increasingly, and let your prayers be heard softly.

The sun doesn't dim its light for those who feel it is shining too bright.
It shines on and those that can't take it find their way to the comfort of the darkness in the shade.

The sun keeps shining, spreading its light to the world. Those who can't take the light find their own comfort in the darkness of shade.

The story can only begin when you dare to turn the page and write.

One look, one gaze, can hold
a thousand unspoken words.

Don't let your heart go unheard.

Trust in the universe and
speak your heart.

Longing
for the moment I can speak the heart's unspoken words.

Waiting
for the moment I can speak of divine stories and destiny.

Knowing
this moment is already written in the stars.

Trusting
in the universe, in my soul, in my heart.

Love is the reason.
Love is the only reason.

Our only purpose is to love,

be love, and

give love.

Love is the meaning of life.

Women are creators and nurturers filled with the energy of the divine feminine. An energy that allows us to be powerful, protective, and loving.

No longer will this energy be hidden, fought, and controlled by society. My women, let your light shine like you are destined to. Together, we will rise; together, we will shine so bright we will light up the world.

I daydream… I dream and dream…
those dreams become my goals and I work to make those goals my reality.

Anything is possible when you remind yourself that you are capable of achieving your dreams.

When your intention is pure, your dreams will become your destiny.

I made a personal vow long ago that I will never compromise my integrity, not for anyone, anything, or any path. What is meant for you never means you must compromise your integrity to achieve your destiny. What is meant for you will always bring you divinity.

Life is not about being perfect.
It is about being so ridiculously passionate
that people either think you're a little crazy
or they take your hand and join you.

6

Love & Gratitude

> Cultivate the habit of
> being grateful for every good
> thing that comes to you, and to
> give thanks continuously.
>
> Ralph Waldo Emerson

Gratitude is magic,

It allows you to
fall in love with
the life you have.

When you are grateful, an energy resonates from your soul. This energy allows you to fall in love with the life you have, your challenges become opportunities, and your heart becomes filled with love, faith, and happiness.

When you can show the universe gratitude for what you have, life reveals even more love, even more happiness, and more abundance to you.

Gratitude is a light from within,
when it shines from your heart.
Love your life, and this light in turn
brings you more love.

Gratitude is alchemy,
it can turn dreams into destiny.
It can turn the unexpected into serendipity.
It can turn a glance into love.
It allows you to shine with a divine light, knowing you are
blessed from above.

Gratitude works like magic...

It can turn a house into a home,

it can turn work into passion,

it can turn challenges into opportunities,

it can turn dreams into destiny,

it can turn the unexpected into serendipity,

it can turn a smile into friendship and

a glance into love.

When you can show the universe gratitude for what you have, life reveals even more love, more happiness, and more abundance to you.

Today, tell someone you love them.

Thank someone for their love, for their friendship.

Show life your gratitude and watch the magic unfold.

Today, tell someone you love them.

Thank someone for their love, for their friendship.

Be grateful,

give love,

be love, and

receive love.

Gratitude unlocks the fullness of life. It turns what we have into more than enough.

It turns denial into acceptance, chaos into order, and confusion into clarity.

It can turn a meal into a feast, a house into a home, a stranger into a friend.

It turns problems into gifts, failures into successes, the unexpected into perfect timing, and mistakes into important events.

It can turn an existence into a real life, and disconnected situations into important and beneficial lessons.

Gratitude makes sense of our past, brings peace for today, and creates a vision for tomorrow.

Gratitude turns negative energy into positive energy.

7

Love & Courage

"Courage is the most important of all the virtues because without courage, you can't practice any other virtue consistently."

Maya Angelou

Crowns are not made of gold and diamonds.

Crowns are made up of courage, conviction,
and confidence.

They shine when the woman believes in herself.

Crowns glimmer with courage, shine with determination,
and are framed with fearlessness.

It's the courage to speak your truth.

It's the confidence to love wildly.

It's the conviction to live untamed.

This is the magic that exists in all of us.

Embrace your magic.

Sitare

She looks up to the stars, seeing her destiny written so beautifully by their light.

Watching each star burn with a passion to bring beauty into the world, even in the darkest night.

She felt inspired and whispered words of gratitude, the stars whispered back to you, will always shine just as bright.

Lost in the magic of illumination, feeling a sense of divination, knowing the stars are shining just for her.

Untamed Part 1

She loves freely and wildly, the power of truth is what guides her, along with the strength of her instinct and the music that plays from her heart.

She will be the one who sets your soul on fire.

Her intuition guides her, the truth protects her and her faith leads the way.

Love Her and she will show you what it means to live with your soul on fire.

Walk with her and you will hear the music her heart dances to.

Hold her hand and she will show you how to live wildly courageous and passionately ambitious.

Behind her smile lies a world of magic, love, and mystery.

Become the flames, a beautiful sight to see, and those standing close will feel the heat from your ambitions burning so passionately.

She flows fiercely, guided by her spirit with passion in her eyes.

She will not be tamed and leaves normal behind.

She loves deeply from her heart and always speaks from her soul.

She reflects the light of the moon and shines like gold.

She walks with confidence.

She smiles with kindness.

She feels magic in the moonlight.

Her soul burns with desire to love and freefall.

She has a passion for life and gives life her all.

8

Love & Alchemy

Express the Love that's in your heart,

Because Love should not be a secret,

It should be shared and set free

And then you will truly see
what's meant to be

As an Alchemist can turn iron into gold,
you can transform your life into your dreams.
All it takes is confidence, courage, and conviction.
Believe in yourself, believe in your rarity with confidence.
Believe in your dreams with purity and courage,
then walk down your chosen path with tenacity and conviction.

You must set yourself free in order to experience the alchemy of life.

You must let go of the molds society has created for you because you were not born to fit into anyone else's definition of you and for you. You were born to stand in your own sense of self and to embrace your rarity.

You must let go of timelines that have been thrust upon you and understand that divine timing is at play. Nothing will come to you too early or too late.

You must not look at others with a sense of envy and try to duplicate the lives of others. The more you look at the lives of others, the more time you have taken away from being your best possible self. The more time you have taken away from this present moment.

The past has passed. Today is the day that you can embrace your rarity, embrace all the unique qualities that make you, YOU. Today is the day that you embrace the present moment and decide to live life differently. Today is the day that you choose love, joy, and happiness over dislike, sadness, and melancholy.

Today is the day you choose alchemy. Today is the day you choose to create the life you desire.

I made a choice a very long time ago
that I would never make a choice that would compromise
my integrity.
My truth and my integrity are the needles on my
internal compass.

On the path towards dreams and soul purpose, one will never have to compromise integrity or sacrifice dignity. If it is meant for you, it will come to you through hard work, passion, and sincerity.

She cannot be bound

The wild woman is intuitive by nature and distinctive by devotion.

No matter what restrictions are placed on her,

No matter what rules are created around her,
She cannot be bound.

There comes a point in time,
where she feels the stir of the wild within her,
the call of the divine feminine from all the goddesses that exist across cultures.
She embraces this energy.
She breaks free.

She runs with wolves,
wildly intuitive and distinctively free,
knowing she shares the same energy.

When you know her for a fleeting moment, you become mad wanting to know more.
Her eyes have a fire that sparks a flame within your soul.

Her soul radiates with the power of love, bliss, and desire.

She can touch the divine.

She will lift you, transform you, and awaken you.

The wild woman shines with the spark of transformation.

She will see you through eyes of pure love and guide you to your highest Self.

She will love the good in you and embrace the dark.

She will teach you about magic and mystery.

She will teach you that what you have settled for before is not enough.

She will speak words that only your heart and soul can understand.

Her aura is ablaze with a love that is so pure it ignites the fire in you.

She will transform you.

Her passion for life and love are flames that can only be fanned, never extinguished. She is always willing to burn for everything that she has ever loved.

She is the divine feminine, and she is unstoppable.

SHE KNOWS...

She knows her power and has stepped into it.

She is wild, playful, and free.

She lives with passion and creativity.

She knows who she is.

She is wisdom.

She is magical.

She is pure love.

She is beautiful.

She is dangerously intuitive.

She is generously loving.

She knows her power and knows that it may intimidate some.

She knows that it will also empower those who are called.

She will stand with you, elevate you, and applaud you.

She knows her power and sees your power.

She knows…

Run Wild with Me

Run wild with me,
dance and be free.
Love unconditionally,
laugh uncontrollably,
run wild with me.

Dance when no one is watching.
Dance when everyone is watching.
Laugh at nothing,
love everything, and
smile from your soul.

Be who your heart wants you to be,
which is divine and free,
without a care about what they think you should be.
Just love endlessly for
love will set you free.

Run wild with me.

They see chaos,

she sees prerogative.

They see crazy,

she sees free-spirited.

They see wild,

she sees free.

She is empowered.

She is awakened.

She draws energy from the earth, the rain, and the wind.

She dances with the stars and

whispers to the moon.

Rebelliously in love with love,

intuition guides her truly, madly, and deeply.

She loves uncontrollably.

She is a free spirit,

wild and untamed,

fearless and unpredictable,

love her and love her wild.

I don't apologize for
the wild in me…

The most powerful thing
you can do is stand up and
show your soul.

Capture my soul,

feel it in my soul,

see it in my eyes, and

feel the love rise

I am the poem

and he is the poet.

I am the ink that flows cosmically

and he is the peacock feather that writes in the stars.

I am a blank page

and love will write its story on me.

Fill your heart with divine love

and you will be surrounded by the colours of joy, passion,

freedom, and

live joyously.

Pure love sets you free

to live surrounded by the colours of passion, music, and

creativity.

Pure love allows you to live joyously.

To live with colour,

to find passion creatively, and

to live with the colours of love

is to live joyously.

She will…

The tamed woman will love you, but she will not set you free.

She will just walk alongside you quietly.

The wild one, the awakened one,

she brings the power of Shakti,

she will embrace your darkness,

she will fill your wounds with light, and

she will love you unconditionally.

She will awaken you and you will not be able to go back to being asleep.

She will set you free magically, passionately, and curiously.

Choose to walk with her but do not try and tame her.

For she is as wild as she is free.

She will encourage you to love freely

and you get to choose, will you set yourself free?

Untamed Part 2

If you choose to walk with me

you choose to accept my heart

as wild,

as it is free.

A free soul cannot and should not be tamed.

Walk with me and I will show you

magic and love.

I will turn your soul into a divine flame that can never be extinguished.

The sun, the moon, the wind, and the sea all carry messages to those whose hearts are untamed, wild, and free.

She is like the wind—she is strong and fierce enough to change the shape of the sand dunes, yet she can be soft like a gentle breeze that seems to whisper love.

9

Love & Poetry

Poetry inspired by Rumi,

The devotion of Meera,

The Love of Radha ,

And embracing the Goddess within

This is a collection of notes written spontaneously as I would gaze at the ocean or get lost in the dance of smoke burning from incense.

Allow it to empower and inspire you!

Allow it to awaken the divine feminine and masculine within!

I just want to be me,

a soulful child at heart,

wild and free.

A woman who believes in Magic,

Love and Destiny.

Someone who will drop everything,

just to watch the leaves dancing

and the rain falling,

pondering the scriptures of Descartes,

dreaming freely,

loving deeply.

I am who I am.

What else can I be?

I wear my heart on my face;

my eyes will always tell you what you need to know.

My silence speaks my truth.

I don't see faces, I feel souls.

I walk through life deeply with my heart and my intuition, and I give my love, loyalty, and protection fully to my loved ones.

I can be gentle as a flower with my love but will be strong as thunder with my morals.

My faith is my everything,
my love keeps me going and
my passion keeps me dancing.

When I dance, I feel like the music becomes the very beat of my heart, and it sets my soul completely free.

Lovers and dreamers alike gaze upon the same moon,
each feeling the same magical moonlight, hearing the
whispers of love and destiny.
The moon will always be
inspiration to poets,
magic to mystics and
enchantment to lovers.

The moon knows all my secrets.

The moon speaks to me about love as I whisper my heart's desire...

Choose to be free to pursue pure love and passion and the universe will light your way.

Live out loud

Dance out loud

Love out loud

The Divine in the Sea

Seashells carry the energy of the ocean

with such emotion

that you can feel the sublime

within the sea and the divine...

Look closely,

you can see the universe in a grain of sand

and divinity in the turquoise waves of the sea.

The waves speak to the sand about unconditional love.

The breeze whispers secrets of destiny to the palm leaves.

When you see with love

and feel with love,

all that surrounds you,

becomes love.

Look closely,

you can feel the warmth of love in the sun.

You can see the universe in a grain of sand,

divinity in the turquoise waves of the sea,

and hear your destiny in the breeze through the palm trees.

My Personal Motto

One must always be sparkly in life and fill the lives around her with a sparkle of love and light.

May your eyes sparkle with love,

your smile sparkle with joy,

your words sparkle with compassion,

and your being sparkle with passion.

I see inspiration in the subtle smoke from incense.

I see love in the moon's luminous incandescence.

These thoughts become my poetry,

magic, love, and mystery.

The Power of Love

Love is the power that creates light.

Love is the power that moves creation.

Love is life.

When love is pure and unconditional, it frees the heart.

When love is divine, it frees the spirit.

Know that you are loved, purely and divinely.

Live life with love.

Have the humility to say I love you

Have the sensitivity to say I need you.

Have the purity to say I think about you.

To live with heart is to live being free.

Live life with love.

Live life with life.

To live is to love,

to love is to live,

to live without love is not life at all.

There is pure love within your heart.

Speak this love,

to thine own self be true,

and then divine love will always embrace you.

There is an enchantment to the soul who loves purely for the sake of love.

Love exists to be spoken and to be given unconditionally.

Allow the love that is within your heart to be set free!

Set free the love that is within your heart!

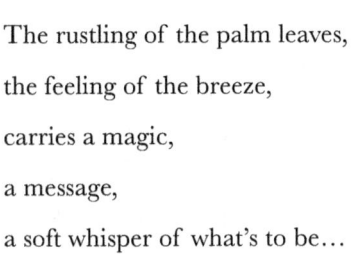

The rustling of the palm leaves,

the feeling of the breeze,

carries a magic,

a message,

a soft whisper of what's to be…

Listening to the rain,

watching the wind bend the trees,

looking out from the middle row,

a connection from another lifetime,

ancient love tied within souls…

Giving

When you give a helping hand,

when you give a warm smile,

when you give to humanity,

you receive love,
abundance, and magic.

Giving with love cures all.

Giving from the heart creates more
love in the world.

The heart that is awakened shines with the light
of a lantern.

There is an enchantment to the soul who loves for the sake of love.

The passion for life allows the heart to ignite and the soul to glow.

Each word of our poetry is like a musical note in this love story.

The notes come together to form this music,
this poetry that writes the story of the heart.

The stories of the heart are poems only you can see.

Each word of our poetry is like a musical note in this love story.

The song that it forms sings sweetly of destiny.

I want that love that makes ocean music,

I want the love of the endless ocean, the sound of no shore.

Because a lover only wants to be in love's presence,

and love only wants to be in love's presence.

My hair is not always perfect and done,

it's usually up in some sort of messy bun.

I always walk with purpose,

but I'm also scatterbrained,

so I trip on nothing,

heels stuck in something,

making me essentially

a walking circus.

But my crown,

my crown is always on.

It's not made of diamonds, pearls, and gold.

No.

It's made of courage,

conviction,

a passionate swirl,

a Fearless twirl,

and a growl that says

this woman's got her crown on.

Rumi says, *devote yourself to your beloved.*

My heart is full of devotion, my soul with knowing, as I await my beloved.
To some it's waiting, to the mystics it's already begun.

I ask my loved ones,
and how is your heart?
Their soul will respond
with love, for love, and
because of love.

I'm weird, I have embraced this fact because I love the fact that I am weird, an oddball,

I do not want to fit in, blend in, or live understated.

I want to be a misfit. I want to blend out. I want to live overstated.

I wouldn't want it any other way because I don't know how to be any other way.

Embrace your weirdness. Embrace every facet of what defines you, for you are a rare gem that is destined to shine. Your glow will light up the world around you, and your joy, living in your deep authenticity and weirdness, will illuminate the path for others.

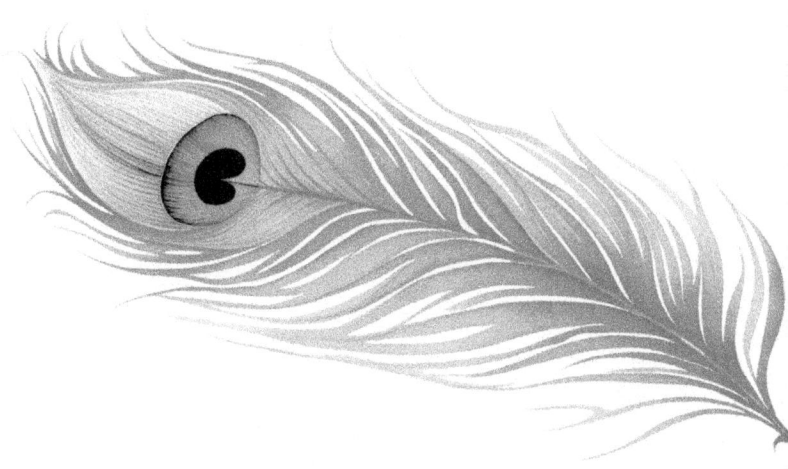

If you live asleep, how can your dreams
be awakened?

If you live asleep, how can you give your
dreams life?

As Krishna is to Radha,
as Manjnu is to Laila,
when love is unconditional,
it becomes a divine love.

Divine love is love from the soul, from the heart, in its purest form. It is love without conditions; it is love for the sake of love.

Our hearts give us rhythm
so life should be danced
freely.

The universe has its own rhythm, and that rhythm is love.
And so, we should dance to it,
passionately,
freely,
lovingly, and
joyously.

True Love

True love allows you to be you. True love brings out the best in you while allowing you to feel safe with your scars. True love says I love the dark because it made you who you are today. And true love then holds your hand as you walk through the light, shining your brightest.

Love is in your destiny.
Love is your only destiny.
Be open to receive it,
be open to become it, and
believe that you are worthy of it.

> "Goodbyes are only for those who love with their eyes. Because for those who love with heart and soul there is no such thing as separation."
>
> Rumi

REFERENCES

Chapter 1

Khan, H. I. (n.d.). Asked for strength. Retrieved from https://www.spiritualityandpractice.com/quotes/quotations/view/21122/spiritual-quotation

The Holy Bible, New International Version. (1984). 1 Corinthians 13:13.

Mother Teresa. (n.d.). "If you judge people, you have no time to love them." [Attributed].

Chapter 2

Thich Nhat Hanh. (1991). *Peace is every step: The path of mindfulness in everyday life.* Bantam Books.

"The present moment is filled with joy and happiness; if you are attentive, you will see it."

Chapter 3

Rumi. (1997). *Rumi: In the arms of the beloved* (Trans. J. Moyne & M. Barks). Shambhala.

"I once had a thousand desires, but in my one desire to know you, all else melted away."

Chapter 4

Oscar Wilde. (n.d.). Unless it is mad, passionate, or extraordinary love, it's a waste of your time. There are too many mediocre things in life; love shouldn't be one of them. [Attributed].

Chapter 5

Paulo Coelho. (2012). *Manuscript found in Accra* (A. J. Costa, Trans.). Knopf.

"The reward for work is not what we get, but what we become."

Chapter 6

Ralph Waldo Emerson. (n.d.). Cultivate the habit of being grateful for every good thing that comes to you, and to give thanks continuously. [Attributed].

Chapter 7

Maya Angelou. (n.d.). Courage is the most important of all the virtues because without courage, you can't practice any other virtue consistently. [Attributed].

Chapter 8

Gupta, R. (2023). *Auspicious: Embracing courage, conviction, and confidence*. Dolce Media Group.

CHAPTER 9

Gupta, R. (2023). *Auspicious: Embracing courage, conviction, and confidence*. Dolce Media Group.

www.ingramcontent.com/pod-product-compliance
Lightning Source LLC
Chambersburg PA
CBHW032225080426
42735CB00008B/717